The Sight You See

Authored by Petar Kostadinov

The Sight You See by Petar Kostadinov © 2014

Published by pajkpublishing.com

FIRST PRINTING

U.S.A

© 2014 by Petar Kostadinov
All rights reserved.   No part of this publication may be reproduced or transmitted in any form by means, electronic or mechanical, including photocopy, recording, or any information storage and retrieval system, without permission in writing from the copyright owner.

In this book some of the poetry is fiction and some are non-fiction. Any resemblance to person, places, events, are pure coincidental.

pajkpublishing
ISBN-13: **978-0615975634** (Custom)
ISBN-10: **0615975631**

Cover Design by Petar Kostadinov (c) 2014

The Sight You See by Petar Kostadinov © 2014

Dedications;

I can't thank enough more than anyone, everyone that still gives me the loving unconditional support to write. My two Son's Alaric and Jaresson; Guys you rule and thanks for your great laughter.

My grandmother Ratka who thought me to read and encouraged me to write and work on my craft as well my parents Jagotka and Vanco, that still giving me the love that starlights my heart.

My readers and my co-workers in Irondequoiut library; Thank you for the support, you are kindness and support on my craft shines with you.

To Love of my Life, you are gift of time and I love you.

The Sight You See by Petar Kostadinov © 2014

Contents;

You are complete song	10
Miles from home	11
Unedited charts	12
Santa clause is coming to town	13
When time speaks	14
Somewhere in time	15
Seatere	16
I am gonna rock you easy tonight	17
Stuck in winter white	18
California	19
There Was....	20
Sense of existence	21
On the day of yesterday	22
Galaxy 6543	23

And time	**24**
Beethoven said;	**25**
They call them heroes	**26**
At Galilee	**27**
C drive	**28**
You are angel	**29**
Your kisses	**30**
You are like a star	**31**
I go on crazy here not having you	**32**
Earths surface	**33**
Time is essence of life	**34**
Perception of life	**35**
The sun is out	**36**
Wonder	**37**
somewhere	**38**
I was born	**39**
my last days	**40**

Timeless treasure	**42**
You keep me heatedly	**43**
My Queen	**44**
God is right	**46**
The way of the golden road	**48**
You are the reason I love	**50**
More than light	**51**
when darkness falls	**53**
After the song	**55**
Timeless star	**57**
time will tell	**58**
Meeting GOD for the first time	**59**
The foggy rainy day	**61**
Knock on the sea	**62**

Thought	**64**
I need you tonight	**65**
Emersing in light	**66**
To you	**69**
If today were my last day	**70**
Times like this	**71**
Knock on the sea	**73**
The road	**75**
Presence in your light	**77**
Give Her The Day	**78**
The road to Everglades	**79**
Once in the song	80
Bathtub	**82**

Vast Universe	83
Where is heaven?	84
City light , Busy lights	85
Space Discovery	87
You can love me just like that	88
Toledo rain	90
Of beautiful heartbeat	93
One Movie	94
New Year	95
Your lips my lips	97
The road 1	98

The Sight You See by Petar Kostadinov © 2014

Notes and Thoughts

You are complete song

Every time I look at you

The world seems brighter

In my sleep

The road seems shinier

Easier lighter

You are complete song

Miles from home

The road tougher

The song lighter

On the sweetest moments

Existence

Lord has me eternity

In precise joy

Glorified seas

Unedited charts

Every song sings
God given glory
Yet story
Makes it perfect
Harmony

Santa clause is coming to town

His bringing sweet joys and sounds
Making sure all is abound
Beautiful miracles jazzy
In our hearts that is shout

When time speaks

As the sea parts
And amist morning comes
The winter moons shones
With that song
We are great peaceful
Miracles
Forever stronger
Forever braver

Somewhere in time

Somewhere in time she waits
As diamonds and pearls
Wave in spring
The rain of rainbow
Churns so sweetly
Here is the song
That makes us all
Complete
She is my queen

Seatere

It should be
That road
To somewhere
Heroes roll
And promises
Of golden times
Swifting through
The night

I am gonna rock you easy tonight

I am gonna rock you easy tonight
Chase you loving you
Sweeter days
Morning paradise

Stuck in winter white

Stuck in winter white
The sun surely hid
From the Christmas
After party eve
Snow plowing
Not complete
So stuck in the middle
As my dad comes by
To help me get out
He did his magical
Professional drive

California

California
Here I come
Hollywood
My sweet days
Movie stars
Chasing a. Dream
Something tells me
I am gonna make it here
Being a great star on
Hollywood boulevard

There Was....

There was a time like these
Beautiful paradise

Sense of existence

Time is a beauty
In itself
The evermore
Journey

On the day of yesterday

On the day of yesterday
The sunsets come away
Longing for your passionate
Kisses never amiss

Time is singing tune
Morning to noon
Midnight to afternoon

Love is just beating drum
Beautiful song ride

Galaxy 6543

The journey of tomorrow
Was the endless light
Beyond existable song
Brimming through the evermore
Glades

And time

And time
Has lasted as long as
The sea has been there
On earthly songs
On majestically cheered lights
The rows of light
Brings out the slightest
Sounds

We are all beknowns
To our diversity
Each of us humanity

Beethoven said;
"I will make them
Rise and dance
So be it
Time to chime
Time to rhyme
This is the beautiful song ride"

They call them heroes

They call them heroes
They zag through the high
Mighty light to save a soul
From the deeper wounds
Peaceful so clear

At Galilee

Once there was one big giant tree
And one day it flew over the sea
It chased the sun at dawn
And it chased the moon at night light

The moon shoned over
To kindly speak up its views
Time told a tale of many great deeds
For one man became a king
Mother Mary was proud of him

Peaceful heart joyful mind
Passage in time he wrote the book
Of humanity humiliation will

C drive

C drive
And a rambling man
Only hope
The diversion of a great song
Love is a hero of our grand Devine
You and I are great light
Such a perfect night
Great melody singing tonight
Just for us eternally
Amazingly

You are angel

You are angel
Sent here from heaven
Makes all perfect sense

Your kisses

Your kisses
Are no longer there
You are not so much
As you chased the sun
To be with me
The sea of songs
Have lights that brim
Indefenetly

Unburdened by your beauty
You once made my heart
Skip a beat of thunder light

You are like a star

You are like a star
That shines through
The sky
You are like a butterfly
That flies through
Those golden fields
That shine so brighter
Making it lighter

I go on crazy here not having you

I go on crazy here not having you
In my arms and this ride is the fiddle
On my mind you are my only
song sung on my heart perfectly
strongly

Earths surface

Rivers and stones

Yesterday's song
Mindful of time

The road is peaceful sign

Time is essence of life

Time is essence of life
Perpetual bliss
Morning of song
Beautiful sunshine key

Perception of life

Perception of life
The guidance

of tomorrow
On miracle light

The sun is out

The sun is out
The rain is gone
It is a beautiful day
Outside to play

wonder

It is the rain

that makes me

wonder

somewhere

somewhere some day
You may come around
Don't look beyond

The days are beautiful
sunrise
Purified sunshine

I was born

I was born to play guitar
Strumming through great lines
All over every peace of mind

my last days

The road has come
For me to sail away
The song that sung
My heart
It is no longer there

I can attest to all
I met and greeted
I am shifting up high
Through the skies
To see those that

The Sight You See by Petar Kostadinov © 2014

I have lost so close to me
Dearly years before eye
lay
In front of me

Timeless treasure

Beyond sunrise
Beyond talkative light
Every musical line
C to A to sharper key
Fuses the journey
That made up the
Stories unbroken ones
You and I are paradise

You keep me heatedly

You keep me warm
Chasing my dreams
Inside my soulful heart
Beating so hard

My Queen

no merit is her song
She dances without a
Doubt in her heartfull
heart
Beautiful as her smile she
is
puts her dancing shoes on
Dances through the night
No storms could stop her

The Sight You See by Petar Kostadinov © 2014

Her sun pushes it with
Her magic no wind could
Blaze her she is stronger
Inside of her

She is Gods of an angel

God is right

turning to page one
The book was written
In rhyme
The story goes on
As to how we must love
another to respect each
other

We are creation by him
Painted in melody

The Sight You See by Petar Kostadinov © 2014

We are no lightning
We are sunrise through that
Haze just beyond the rain

He spoke to me many times
I rose up to listen to him
His wise words were so much
Heartedly helpful

When I needed his help
He was there he is there
God is always right
And right beside my heart

The way of the golden road

These are memories I cherish

These are dreams I make up to be

coming on reality

These are the songs that cradle my

Heart rolling faithfully

Times are there for all of us

To relax reminisce how it use to be

feeling ageless not grayer

Use to jive a long hair

Now I have none but a prayer

You are the reason I love

You are the reason I love
You are the reason I care
Treasure by treasure
You are my only one

Precious times I love
Sweeter lighter sense

More than light

The song has found it's time
There in the richest distance
No dust nor particle of mighty
Journey that fuels the grounds
It possesses the peaceful sounds
Whether it is bound

Whether it is loud
Not a shout nor shout

Flowerily clouds

when darkness falls

When darkness falls
you get up stronger
You put your smile
Forward with peaceful
Morning

You pose with God
Because he is your
Guiding light

Tornadoes in your heart
Know that somehow
It all goes to show you are
Sound in your mind

After the song

After life
After light
After the ride
The song has it
Glowing flowing
Growing
Evermore drawing
Peacefully plowing

Diversifying
After the song
Shining

Timeless star

It finds itself
By the memorized
Light for the kingdom
Has starred where
No creature has
succumbed
As if then they must
For solitude in their hearts

time will tell

The road has it so
The moment of hello
The untraceable song
Beyond the breathable light

Meeting GOD for the first time

where was the sign?
I imagined it had been
Hidden in the light
Behind the fine art
Dear lord has painted
His heart was pure
His song was mure

At the passage of yesterday
The ringing bells said hurray

The foggy rainy day

Like a mirror
Like a light
Like a brief
Sweeter passage
Written on a stone
Older as time
Older as any golden star
Chasing around its sunlight

Knock on the sea

to be exact
At after sea light
The song of sounds
After midnight
two precise knocks
I hear mostly
Chasing to what appears
Some kind of ghostly

The Sight You See by Petar Kostadinov © 2014

This burden of a fear
Now should I sleep?
Could not close my eyes
Feeling uneasy about it all
Through this night

Thought

A process of creation
Thought great good
hearted
Peaceful light surrounds it
With its remarkable wings
Wider and wiser spread
Around its mysterious
journey
You and I are perfect story
Perfect history

I need you tonight

I need you tonight
You are a blessed light
Tomorrow is another
Song ride

Emersing in light

The road has taken upon me
Six to seven a week
The years has made my
Hairline gray
I have aged as you can see
"Old man and the sea" I seek
To feel some kind of breeze
Just as the song has begun
To sing it surely feels unreal

The Sight You See by Petar Kostadinov © 2014

Without its morning light
Time is bound to fly by

I seek those that are heroes
To heal my soul for I need not be
So sad inside my heartbeat
Tomorrow if I lean to be with my lord
I will look down to help those in need be
for when they sorrow fearlessly

Now I look upon high seas
Change my mind to beat
the
Drum

Like many a human
Of one breed
Flash bones blood
I am no machine
Time will surely tell

To you

Just is tonight
To you obviously
I am song bound free
To twinkle in the sea

If today were my last day

If today were my last song

The clock would tick twice

in one beat

If today the rain would

make me sing

like a king

for the little bit

of everything I am

Times like this

Chasing the moon rise
Chasing the sunrise wide open
To me this is life
Seating and waiting on love
stop tormenting me and my heart
Coffee would do the trick
Tea would embrace my song inside of me

Every day is true paradise
Admiring you from a glance

Knock on the sea

to be exact

At after sea light

The song of sounds

After midnight

two precise knocks

I hear mostly

Chasing to what appears

Some kind of ghostly

This burden of a fear

Now should I sleep?

Could not close my eyes

Feeling uneasy about it all

Through this night

The road

Tonight I gaze upon

Each star as though

The return of god's son

Shines bright

I feel so purified inside

of me

I am just a human being

Creature that has brains

Two hands two feet

Ears mouth nose

Eyes that see everything

That surrounds me

Presence in your light

The pure emotion

The starlight peace

With the remenece time

We are one guiding

pride

Give Her The Day

Give her day to her

Everything for her is

Grateful

Golden as she is in

sunshine

In Written Skies

Bells are ringing

The road to Everglades

The song to midnight train

The peaceful river streams

Once in the song

Once has been the in

the song

That yearned for the

light

To shine immensely

As sweeter as coprikine

As dandelion treasures

Of to the gondiline

The Sight You See by Petar Kostadinov © 2014

Of to the mystified

In the journey for it be

The years are so sweet

Bathtub

Self absorbing bathtub

When someone takes a shower

Vast Universe

The universe is here

The song is dear

Where is heaven?

Down below my heart

Beating

Above my time shifting

City light, Busy lights

The streamline

Of time as they all

Rush by

Busy to work and from

Tourists touring its beautiful

Sight

The bright full songs

From birds music

You hear cars rushing by

People relaxed in Bryant park

Next to the central library

Sitting statue of the real glacier

of

Mr Bryant himself reading a

book in his hands

In New York City

Such a beauty

Such a time full pride

In each and every heart

Space Discovery

Ultimate

adventure

skyrocket

You can love me just like that

The pieces of my life

The sweet touch

That you give to my

heart

That smile you river me

I am stronger

The Sight You See by Petar Kostadinov © 2014

You are daisy queen

Pure and so real

You can love me

Just like that

Not a day goes by

Toledo rain

(Chorus)

Sunshine through

The skies

Cloud number twenty

nine

Laughing at my heart

Here u are here I am

When the rain falls

We are just as good

As number one track

On my mind

Toledo rain

Tornado falls

Looking in

I pass on by

This is a good ride

Any day now

We are so much more

The sun will peel (peek) through

The uneven side of us

(Repeat chorus)

Of beautiful heartbeat

If you want to say a word

In heaven you are the angels

light that shines through the sea

Of beautiful heartbeat

One Movie

One Movie

One Script

One beautiful Story

First time

In this world

Beautiful as you are

In your heart

The Sunshine Shining

Godly

New Year

Spoken New Words

Spoken New Songs

New rivers New

passages

The Sight You See by Petar Kostadinov © 2014

On old days that has

been right

Everything forgotten

Like a dust

Your lips my lips

Sweet times

Just like these

Perfect harmony

Perfect memories

The road 1

Has its lines

Heavy rains

Six tails

To know more about the Author and his books please visit

http://petarkostadinov.webs.com/

The Sight You See by Petar Kostadinov © 2014

Notes And Thoughts

The Sight You See by Petar Kostadinov © 2014

Notes and Thoughts

www.ingramcontent.com/pod-product-compliance
Lightning Source LLC
Chambersburg PA
CBHW071742090426
42738CB00011B/2537